National Audit Office

AF885306

Royal Household spending and accountability

The Royal Household

Report by the Comptroller and Auditor General

Ordered by the House of Commons
to be printed on 12 July 2023

This report has been prepared under Section 6 of the National Audit Act 1983 for presentation to the House of Commons in accordance with Section 9 of the Act

Gareth Davies
Comptroller and Auditor General
National Audit Office

6 July 2023

HC 1661 | £10.00

Value for money reports

Our value for money reports examine government expenditure in order to form a judgement on whether value for money has been achieved. We also make recommendations to public bodies on how to improve public services.

012734 07/23 NAO

Contents

This report can be found on the National Audit Office website at www.nao.org.uk

If you need a version of this report in an alternative format for accessibility reasons, or any of the figures in a different format, contact the NAO at enquiries@nao.org.uk

The National Audit Office study team consisted of:

Leon Bardot, Alysia Hill, Heather James, Brian Kennedy, Esther Namukasa, Naseem Ramjan and Ralph Ross Camelo, with assistance from Matthew Caine and Farhan Subhan, under the direction of Sian Jones.

For further information about the National Audit Office please contact:

National Audit Office
Press Office
157–197 Buckingham Palace Road
Victoria
London
SW1W 9SP

020 7798 7400

www.nao.org.uk

@NAOorguk

Key facts

£86.3mn

the value of the Sovereign Grant (the Grant), the main source of public funding for the Royal Household, in 2023-24

£10.1mn

the value of the Sovereign Grant Reserve (the Reserve), a fund where surplus funds are kept for future contingencies, as at 31 March 2023

£117.3mn

the Royal Household's expenditure on official duties and the maintenance of the Occupied Royal Palaces in 2022-23, of which £107.5 million came from public funds (the Grant and the Reserve)

£9.8 million	other income that supplements the Grant. This includes facilities management fees from the Royal Collection Trust, recharges and property rental income
2012	the year the Sovereign Grant Act 2011 (the Act) came into force, replacing the previous funding system for the Royal Household with the Grant
15%	the original percentage of The Crown Estate's revenue account profit that was allocated annually to the Royal Household in the form of the Grant, according to the Act
25%	the updated percentage of The Crown Estate's revenue account profit that is allocated annually to the Royal Household in the form of the Grant, from 2017-18, to fund the reservicing of Buckingham Palace, following the first periodic review of the Grant
£442.6 million	The Crown Estate's revenue account profit in 2022-23, that is deposited into the government's general bank account, known as the Consolidated Fund
£369 million	the total amount approved by HM Treasury to fund the reservicing of Buckingham Palace over a 10-year period from 2017-18
£185.1 million	the amount spent on the reservicing of Buckingham Palace as of 31 March 2023
2023	the most recent periodic review of the Grant is scheduled to be published. If needed, a statutory instrument will be laid in Parliament to adjust the funding formula for the Grant

Summary

1 The Royal Family is funded by a variety of private and public sources. The Royal Household, which supports the Sovereign and members of the Royal Family in their official duties, has been publicly funded since 1760, when King George III agreed to surrender to Parliament the net income from The Crown Estate (see **Figure 1** on pages 6 and 7) and hereditary revenues in return for a fixed annual payment.

2 The Sovereign Grant Act 2011 (the Act) came into force from 1 April 2012. It sets out the approach to calculating the value of the grant paid by HM Treasury to the Royal Household to support the official duties of the Sovereign and to maintain the Occupied Royal Palaces. Prior to this, the government provided financial support to the Sovereign via the Civil List, a payment to cover official expenses, and three additional grants to cover travel, communication and property maintenance.

3 The Sovereign Grant (the Grant) is the source of public funding for the Sovereign. The Sovereign also receives other income from the Privy Purse, including private income from the Duchy of Lancaster. The activities of the Prince of Wales and his family are largely funded by private income from the Duchy of Cornwall.

4 The purpose of this report is to enhance transparency in a matter of national interest. It is not a value-for-money assessment and does not contain recommendations. This report describes the funding arrangements for the Royal Household as well as the accountability and oversight procedures. It outlines:

- the role of public money in financing the Royal Household and how the funds are used (Part One);
- the respective roles of HM Treasury, Parliament and the Comptroller and Auditor General (the C&AG) in providing the funds, engaging in oversight and auditing the accounts (Part Two); and
- future considerations that might impact upon funding for the Royal Household (Part Three).

5 This report focuses on public funding for the Royal Household. It also outlines the accountability arrangements that Parliament has put in place for the duchies of Lancaster and Cornwall, but does not go into detail about the duchies, or other private funds, which are outside of the remit of the National Audit Office (NAO). Appendix One sets out our audit approach and evidence base. Appendix Two sets out the legislation that this report refers to and Figure 1 provides definitions for key terms used in this report.

Figure 1
Definitions of key terms used in this report

We refer to the following terms relating to the Royal Household in our report

Term	Definition
Consolidated Fund	The UK government's general bank account held at the Bank of England. Taxation and other monies paid to HM Treasury are paid into this fund, including the revenue account profit from The Crown Estate.
The Crown Estate	An independent commercial business, set up by the Crown Estate Act 1961, to manage land and the seabed around England, Wales and Northern Ireland. It is a non-financial public corporation with a wide portfolio of investments managed on behalf of the government. It is not the personal property of the Sovereign, and His Majesty receives no monies directly from it. Any revenue account profit from The Crown Estate is paid each year to HM Treasury.
The Crown Estate's revenue account profit	The revenue account profit is stated in the statement of accounts certified by the Comptroller and Auditor General under section 2 of The Crown Estate Act 1961. The revenue account is separate from the capital account. The Sovereign Grant Act 2011 and subsequent Sovereign Grant and Sovereign Grant Reserve annual reports and accounts refer to the revenue account profit as 'income account net surplus'. In 2022-23, the revenue account profit was £442.6 million.
Duchy of Cornwall	Established by Edward III in 1337 as a private estate to provide independence to his son and heir, the Duke of Cornwall. As such, the Duke is entitled to the estate revenue but not the capital assets. The revenue account surplus from the estate goes to the Duke of Cornwall (or the Sovereign when there is no Duke).
Duchy of Lancaster	A portfolio of land, property and assets held in trust for present and future Sovereigns and created as a private estate in 1461.
Head of State	The British Monarchy is a constitutional monarchy, whereby the Sovereign is politically impartial and exercises their constitutional powers on the advice of government ministers. As Head of State, the Sovereign undertakes ceremonial and constitutional duties.
Keeper of the Privy Purse	The Keeper of the Privy Purse and Treasurer to the Sovereign has overall responsibility for the management of the Sovereign's financial affairs. As part of the role, they serve as the Accounting Officer of the Sovereign Grant and are accountable to HM Treasury and to Parliament. The Keeper is appointed by the Sovereign and appointed Accounting Officer for the Sovereign Grant by HM Treasury.
Lord Chamberlain's Committee	The committee responsible for overall management and oversight of the Royal Household's activities, setting strategic plans and priorities, monitoring risk and ensuring that the Royal Household's obligations relating to the Sovereign Grant and to other stakeholders are met.
Occupied Royal Palaces	Buckingham Palace, St James's Palace, the residential and office areas of Kensington Palace, Clarence House, the Royal Mews and Royal Paddocks at Hampton Court and Windsor Castle and buildings in the Home Park at Windsor. This does not include the Historic Royal Palaces, a charity tasked with conserving non-occupied palaces such as the Tower of London and Hampton Court Palace.
Privy Purse	The private finances and estates of the Sovereign. It funds official expenditure incurred by other members of the Royal Family who perform official duties that is not met by the Sovereign Grant, at the discretion of the Sovereign.

Figure 1 *continued*

Definitions of key terms used in this report

Term	Definition
Reservicing of Buckingham Palace	A 10-year project to replace the ageing services (plumbing, electrics, heating and drainage) of the Palace to reduce the risk of fire or flood and deliver operational improvements.
Royal Collection Trust	Royal Collection Trust incorporates a registered charity, the Royal Collection Trust, and its trading company, Royal Collection Enterprises Ltd. It looks after the Royal Collection and manages the public opening of the official residences of the Sovereign in England and Scotland.
Royal Household	Five collective departments that support the Sovereign and members of the Royal Family: the Private Secretary's Office, the Privy Purse and Treasurer's Office, the Master of the Household's Department, the Lord Chamberlain's Office and Royal Collection Trust.
Royal Trustees	The Prime Minister, the Chancellor of the Exchequer and the Keeper of the Privy Purse.
Sovereign Grant	Funds provided by the UK government to support the Sovereign in his official duties, including the maintenance of the Occupied Royal Palaces. The Sovereign Grant replaced the Civil List and grants-in-aid in 2012.
Sovereign Grant Reserve	A fund where surplus funds are held for future contingencies and future expenditure on the Buckingham Palace reservicing programme until its completion.

Source: National Audit Office literature review

Key findings

Funding and expenses

6 **The Royal Household receives public funding in line with the Act**. The Act specifies that the Sovereign receives a grant each financial year. The Grant is used to fund expenditure incurred by the Sovereign and provide certain resources to support other members of the Royal Family in the performance of official duties. This includes staff salaries and travel expenses, as well as maintenance of the Occupied Royal Palaces, including Buckingham Palace and Windsor Castle, which are used for official purposes. Under the Act, the Grant is based on a percentage of The Crown Estate's revenue account profit in the year two years prior to the funding year. The funding formula keeps the Grant in line with the income growth achieved by The Crown Estate. It also guarantees the Grant will not drop below the previous year's funding. For example, in determining the Grant level for 2023-24, 25% of The Crown Estate's 2021-22 revenue account profit, which had dropped during the COVID-19 pandemic, would be £78.2 million, so the Grant was set at the previous year's level of £86.3 million (paragraphs 1.2 and 1.6, and Figures 3 and 4).

7 **The Royal Trustees (the Trustees) determine the annual value of the Grant.** The Trustees are the Prime Minister, the Chancellor of the Exchequer and the Keeper of the Privy Purse, the last of whom is responsible for the day-to-day operations and management of the Grant. The Act requires the Trustees to prepare a yearly report stating the proposed level of the Grant for the following year and how that amount has been determined. Following every five-year period, they must also produce a comprehensive review, including an assessment of what percentage of The Crown Estate's revenue account profit should be used to determine the Grant for the next five-year period. The Act also sets out procedures for adjusting the value of the Grant. HM Treasury must lay a draft statutory instrument before Parliament for the specified percentage. An increase in the percentage would require the statutory instrument to be debated and approved by the House of Commons before the amendment comes into law when the final statutory instrument is laid. A decrease in the percentage can be approved by Parliament without debate (paragraphs 1.6, 1.8 and 1.9).

8 **The Sovereign Grant Reserve (the Reserve) holds unused funds from the Grant.** If the whole of the Grant is not spent for that year, the surplus is paid into the Reserve, controlled by the Trustees. The Royal Household may draw down on the Reserve in future years subject to agreement by the Trustees. The amount that may accumulate in the Reserve is limited in line with the provisions set out in the Act. This gives the Trustees the power to set a lower level of the Grant than the formula would otherwise generate, to encourage a drawdown from the Reserve. The Reserve grew from 2017-18 to 2019-20 when the reservicing of Buckingham Palace was in its early stages and has decreased as the reservicing has progressed. At 31 March 2023, the Reserve held £10.1 million (paragraphs 1.7 and 1.15, and Figure 3).

9 **In 2017, the percentage of The Crown Estate's revenue account profit that should be used to calculate the Grant was increased to fund the reservicing of Buckingham Palace.** The Act originally set the Grant to be 15% of The Crown Estate's revenue account profit for the first five years. The first periodic review by the Trustees, in 2016, recommended that the percentage be increased to 25% from 2017-18. This increase was to fund the reservicing of Buckingham Palace, a 10-year programme. Parliament approved this increase to fund an expected expenditure of £369 million over the life of the programme to 2026-27. By 31 March 2023, £185.1 million had been spent on the programme. The Trustees' 2016 report noted the government's intention to bring forward legislation to reset the level of the Grant to appropriate levels once the reservicing works have been completed (paragraphs 1.10 to 1.14, and Figures 4, 5 and 6).

10 In 2022-23, the Grant was £86.3 million. Of that total, £51.8 million was intended for core activities and £34.5 million for the reservicing of Buckingham Palace. The Royal Household's expenditure on official duties and the maintenance of the Occupied Royal Palaces in 2022-23 amounted to £117.3 million. The Royal Household received £9.8 million from other income including property rentals and recharges for shared services to Royal Collection Trust and the Privy Purse. Funds from the Reserve were used to make up the £21.2 million difference between income and expenditure. HM Treasury expected that the Royal Household would pay into the Reserve during the early stages of the reservicing and would withdraw from the Reserve as the programme progressed (paragraphs 1.15 and 1.16, Figures 4, 7 and 8).

11 The Royal Household's biggest expenditure is property maintenance of the Occupied Royal Palaces. Of the £117.3 million expenditure in 2022-23, 49% (£57.8 million) was spent on maintenance and 23% (£27.1 million) on salaries for employees of the Royal Household who support the work of the Sovereign in their role of Head of State. Most of the maintenance expenditure was spent on the reservicing of Buckingham Palace (£43.0 million). The Royal Household has a rolling ten-year plan for maintaining the Occupied Royal Palaces. Each year, this is broken down to create an annual works programme funded by the Grant (paragraph 1.17 and Figure 8).

Accountability and oversight

12 HM Treasury is the Royal Household's sponsoring department and is therefore responsible to Parliament for the Grant. The Grant is included in HM Treasury's budget. As such, it is responsible for paying the Grant to the Royal Household and ensuring that it complies with all necessary requirements. HM Treasury appoints the Accounting Officer of the Grant, specifies the format of annual report and accounts and has a framework agreement relating to the Grant that sets out the governance and accountability arrangements between HM Treasury and the Royal Household. This agreement also specifies the responsibilities of the Permanent Secretary to the Treasury, the Treasury Officer of Accounts, and the Keeper of the Privy Purse (paragraphs 2.11 to 2.18 and Figure 12).

13 The Keeper of the Privy Purse and Treasurer to the Sovereign (the Keeper) is the Accounting Officer of the Grant and is accountable to HM Treasury and to Parliament. The Keeper is responsible for ensuring that Royal Household spending complies with all relevant legislation and accepted public sector principles, such as propriety and regularity. The Keeper is also required to ensure that they meet the requisite standards of governance, decision-making, transparency and financial management. Under the Act, the Keeper is also required to prepare annual accounts detailing how the Grant was spent and must supply a copy to the C&AG for audit. The Keeper delegates authority to the executive members of the Lord Chamberlain's Committee, which operates as the executive board for the Royal Household, to make decisions and spend up to pre-set limits (paragraphs 2.2 to 2.4).

14 Under the Act, the C&AG, the head of the NAO, audits, certifies and reports on the Grant. The C&AG's audit certificate and report is published within the Sovereign Grant and Sovereign Grant Reserve annual report and accounts each year. The C&AG also carries out value-for-money reviews, which are examinations into economy, efficiency and effectiveness. The NAO previously reported on the Grant and its financial management in 2013. The C&AG plans to undertake value-for-money audit work on the Buckingham Palace reservicing programme in 2024 (paragraphs 2.18 and 2.20).

15 Other income streams received by specific members of the Royal Family, are not subject to the same accountability arrangements as the Grant. As neither the Duchy of Lancaster nor the Duchy of Cornwall are funded by public money, they are not audited by the NAO. However, under the Duchies of Lancaster and Cornwall (Accounts) Act 1838, the accounts of both estates are laid before Parliament. This is facilitated by HM Treasury. Both sets of accounts are audited by privately appointed external auditors. The Treasury Officer of Accounts issues accounts directions to both Duchies, which stipulate the format and accounting standards for the accounts and a minister is required to lay both signed accounts before Parliament. HM Treasury holds an additional statutory layer of oversight over the Duchy of Cornwall to ensure that the long-term value of the estate is not compromised. The Duchy is required to obtain approval from HM Treasury for capital transactions above a set value, which was £0.5 million during 2022-23 (paragraphs 1.20, 1.21, 2.26 and 2.29).

Future considerations

16 Expected revenue related to offshore windfarms is likely to affect the periodic adjustment in the funding formula for the Grant. In January 2023, The Crown Estate signed Agreements for Lease on the latest round of offshore windfarms (Offshore Wind Leasing Round 4 or 'Round 4') and as a result has now started to include the option fee income in its accounts. These fees are expected to significantly increase The Crown Estate's net revenue and revenue account profit. Approximately £1 billion of income per annum will be generated from the option fees across the six projects that comprise Round 4, for at least three years during the option fee period. Since the Grant is set in relation to The Crown Estate's revenue account profit, the Grant would likely increase substantially if the formula is not revised. The latest periodic review of the Grant by the Trustees is expected to be published in 2023 (paragraphs 3.1 to 3.11, and Figure 13).

Part One

Funding and expenditure

1.1 This part sets out:

- the Royal Household's public and private income streams;
- how the Sovereign Grant (the Grant) is calculated;
- the Royal Household's expenditure, particularly what public funds are spent on; and
- an explanation of royal-related activities that are funded by other government departments.

1.2 The Sovereign receives income from a mix of public funding and private income (**Figure 2** on pages 12 and 13). The private income is known as the Privy Purse. The main source of public funding is the Grant. The stated purpose of the Grant is to provide resources for use by the Royal Household in support of His Majesty's official duties as Sovereign. These include:

- salaries for employees of the Royal Household who support and oversee the work of the Sovereign in their role of Head of State;
- the maintenance of the Occupied Royal Palaces, which are used for formal entertaining and ceremonial events;[1]
- travel for official engagements in the UK and overseas undertaken by the Sovereign and other members of the Royal Family acting on his behalf; and
- the royal programme of events, including receptions, dinners, and investitures to celebrate achievements and British culture.

1 The Occupied Royal Palaces are Buckingham Palace, St James's Palace, the residential and office areas of Kensington Palace, Clarence House, the Royal Mews and Royal Paddocks at Hampton Court and Windsor Castle and buildings in the Home Park at Windsor.

Figure 2

Sources of income for the Royal Family

The Royal Household receives both private and public funding

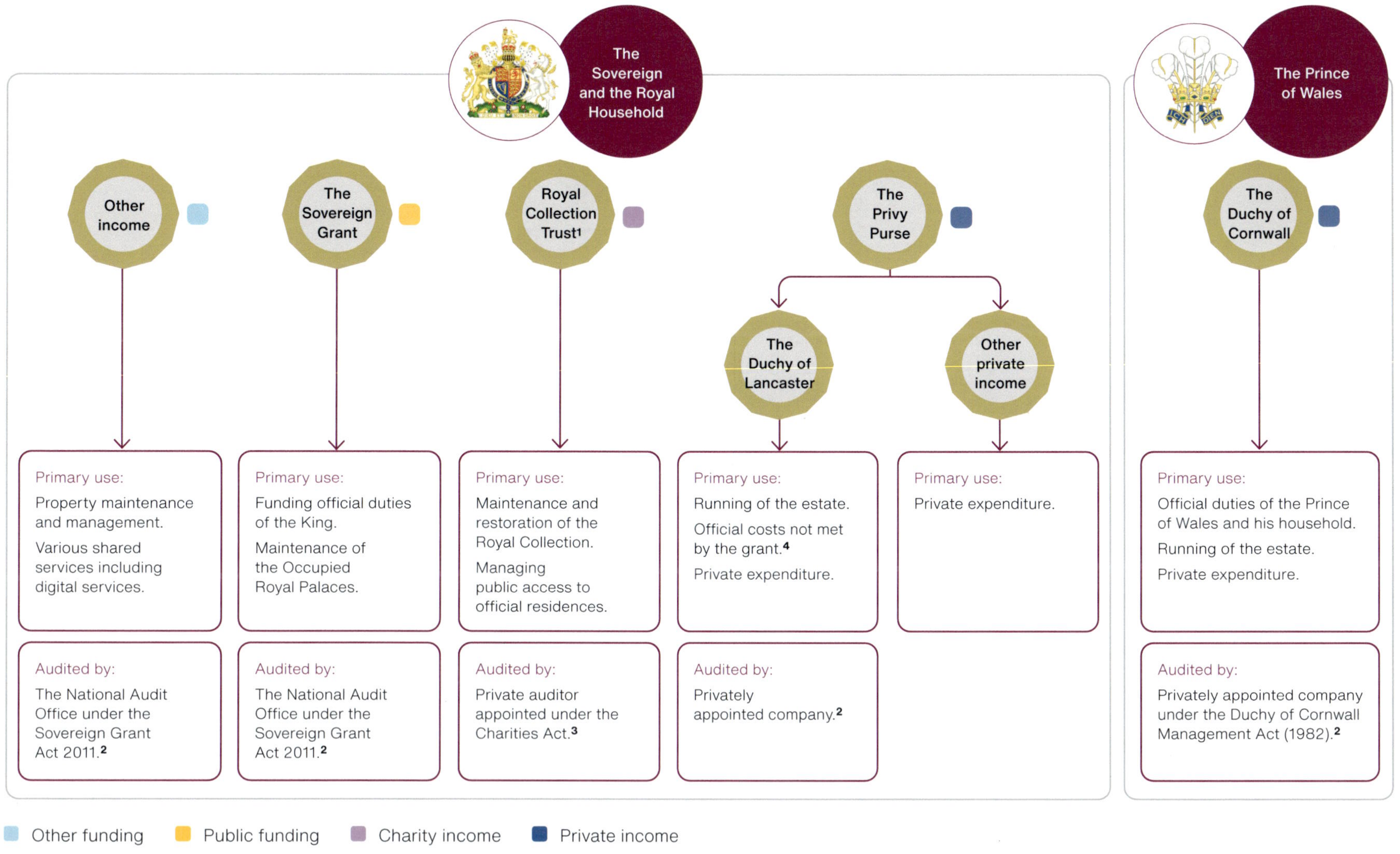

Figure 2
Sources of income for the Royal Family

Notes

1 The Royal Collection Trust is a charity regulated by the Charities Commission. The Trust's income is used to support its charitable purposes.

2 The annual report and accounts for the Sovereign Grant (the Grant) and Sovereign Grant Reserve, the Duchy of Lancaster and the Duchy of Cornwall are all laid in Parliament once they are certified by their auditor.

3 The annual report and accounts for the Royal Collection Trust is not laid in Parliament as it is not accountable to Parliament but is provided to Companies House and the Charity Commission.

4 Income from the Duchy of Lancaster is also used to fund official costs not met by the Grant, including expenditure by members of the Royal Family incurred in the performance of official duties, at the discretion of the Sovereign.

Source: National Audit Office analysis of published annual report and accounts

1.3 The official activities of the Sovereign and the Royal Household have been publicly funded since 1760, when King George III agreed to surrender the profit from The Crown Estate to Parliament in return for an annual payment. By 2011, public funds were provided via two broad streams of income. The Civil List was a payment that funded the Sovereign's official activities. Three separate grants-in-aid were also provided annually by departments for specific purposes. The Department for Transport provided a grant to cover travel. The Department for Culture, Media & Sport provided a grant for maintenance of the Occupied Royal Palaces and another for communications and information.

1.4 The Sovereign Grant Act 2011 (the Act) streamlined funding arrangements by replacing the Civil List and grants-in-aid with a single grant, which was first paid in 2012. We reported in 2013 about the new system, noting that it offered greater certainty over future funding while also providing flexibility in how the Royal Household allocated its spending.[2]

1.5 The Grant is set by reference to a proportion of the revenue account profit of The Crown Estate. While the Crown Estate has existed in some form for hundreds of years, the current arrangements were set in the Crown Estate Act 1961. This Crown Estate Act established The Crown Estate as a business (body corporate) and specifies certain distinctions between capital and revenue to the effect that The Crown Estate resembles a trust. The capital of The Crown Estate is preserved for the Sovereign and his or her successors. However, the income generated from the management of The Crown Estate, minus expenses and transfers, is paid to the Exchequer, into the Consolidated Fund, the government's general bank account, using a structured repayment process agreed with HM Treasury. The Crown Estate is not allowed to borrow money. However, it is allowed to transfer a proportion of its yearly revenue from its revenue account to its capital account to cover the expenses of capital investments. This is currently set at 27% of revenue.

2 Report by Comptroller and Auditor General, *The Sovereign Grant*, Session 2013-14, HC 722, National Audit Office, October 2013.

How the value of the Grant is calculated

1.6 The Royal Trustees (the Trustees) determine the annual value of the Grant. The Trustees are a body established by section 10 of the Civil List Act 1952 as confirmed by section 13(7) of the Sovereign Grant Act. They comprise the Prime Minister, the Chancellor of the Exchequer and the Keeper of the Privy Purse, the last of whom is responsible for the day-to-day operations and management of the Grant. The Sovereign Grant Act sets out in legislation the process that the Trustees must follow to calculate the Grant each year (**Figure 3**). It specifies that the Grant must be calculated as a percentage of The Crown Estate's revenue account profit for the financial year that began two years before the beginning of the relevant financial year but should also not fall below the previous year's value.[3] For example, in determining the Grant level for 2023-24, 25% of The Crown Estate's 2021-22 revenue account profit, which had dropped during the COVID-19 pandemic, would be £78.2 million, so the Grant was set at the previous year's level of £86.3 million.

1.7 If the whole of the Grant is not spent each year, the surplus is paid into a reserve fund, the Sovereign Grant Reserve (the Reserve), controlled by the Trustees. These funds may be drawn down in future years as required, with agreement from the Trustees. The amount that may accumulate in the Reserve is limited in line with the provisions set out in the Act (see step 4 of Figure 3). This gives the Trustees the power to set a lower level of the Grant than the formula would otherwise generate, to encourage a drawdown from the Reserve.

1.8 Each financial year the Trustees prepare a report stating the amount of the Grant for the following financial year and explaining how that amount was set. This report is published after the Sovereign Grant and Sovereign Grant Reserve annual report and accounts and The Crown Estate annual report and accounts for the previous year are published. This report must be provided to HM Treasury and laid before Parliament.

1.9 An increase in the percentage requires a draft statutory instrument to be laid, debated and approved by the House of Commons before the amendment comes into law when the final statutory instrument is laid. A decrease in the percentage can be approved by Parliament without debate. The Act provides additional provision for reducing the value of the Grant, specifically where the Duke of Cornwall (the male heir to the throne) is under the age of 18 for a period of any financial year. In that circumstance, 90% of the Duchy of Cornwall's income is provided to the Sovereign and HM Treasury would reduce the Grant by an equivalent amount. The Act also sets out a requirement for the Trustees to produce a comprehensive review of the Grant, including an assessment of the percentage used to determine the Grant, following every five-year period. The Trustees give a copy of their report to HM Treasury, who must lay a copy before Parliament.

3 The Sovereign Grant Act 2011 and subsequent Sovereign Grant and Sovereign Grant Reserve annual reports and accounts refer to the revenue account profit as 'income account net surplus'.

Figure 3

How the Sovereign Grant (the Grant) is calculated

The Royal Trustees follow a five-step process when calculating the Grant

Step 1

Calculate the requisite percentage of The Crown Estate's profit in the base year.[1]

For 2023-24:
25% of The Crown Estate's revenue account profit in 2021-22 (£312,700,000) was £78,175,000.

Step 2

Round up the value to the nearest £100,000.

For 2023-24:
£78,175,000 was rounded up to £78,200,000.

Step 3

Compare with the previous year's Grant and take the higher value.

For 2023-24:
The value of the Grant in 2022-23 was higher (£86,300,000) than the value generated by Step 2 and therefore the 2022-23 value was taken.

Step 4

Check the Grant Reserve was less than half of the audited net relevant resources in the base year.[2]

For 2023-24:
The value of the fund in 2021-22 (£30,800,000) was less than half of the audited net relevant resources in 2021-22 (£102,400,000) and therefore no action was necessary.

Step 5

Set the Grant amount for the upcoming year.

For 2023-24:
The Grant amount for 2023-24 was set at £86,300,000.

Notes

1 The base year is the financial year that began two years before the beginning of the relevant financial year.

2 The Crown Estate's revenue account profit is called 'income account net surplus' in the Sovereign Grant Act 2011 (the Act) and the yearly reports of the Royal Trustees.

3 The amount that may accumulate in the Sovereign Grant Reserve (the Reserve) is limited in line with the provisions set out in the Act. This provision gives the Royal Trustees the power to set a lower level of the Grant than the formula would otherwise generate, to encourage a drawdown from the Reserve.

Source: National Audit Office analysis of the *Report of the Royal Trustees on the Sovereign Grant 2023-24*

1.10 **Figure 4** shows The Crown Estate's revenue account profit and the value of the Grant over time. The Act originally set the Grant to be 15% of The Crown Estate's revenue account profit. Following the first periodic review by the Trustees in 2016, the percentage was increased to 25% in 2017-18. This increase was to fund the reservicing of Buckingham Palace, a 10-year programme. The 2017 change was enshrined in law via the Sovereign Grant Act 2011 (Change of Percentage) Order 2017. This increase is intended to be temporary until the programme is completed (see paragraph 1.13).

Reservicing Buckingham Palace

1.11 Since 2017, the Royal Household has been undertaking a 10-year reservicing of Buckingham Palace. The framework agreement between the Royal Household and HM Treasury (see paragraphs 2.11 to 2.14) requires that the Occupied Royal Palaces be maintained as buildings of State to a standard that is consistent with the operational needs of the Royal Household as well as the royal, architectural and historic character of the buildings. The Royal Household and HM Treasury determined this reservicing was necessary due to the risk of fire and flood within Buckingham Palace. In keeping with that requirement, the Royal Household commissioned a team of heritage specialists to deliver an options appraisal report in July 2016, with four options for the reservicing of Buckingham Palace: full decant, full occupation, significant occupation, and partial occupation (**Figure 5** on page 18). The report considered the whole-life cost (net present cost) of each option, factoring in the length of construction period.

1.12 The Royal Household eliminated the full decant and full occupation options as too expensive and too lengthy respectively. The Royal Household conducted further analysis of the significant occupation and partial occupation options and concluded that a hybrid of the two options, a 10-year phased refit, would be the preferable course of action given the operational requirements of Buckingham Palace.

1.13 In 2017-18, HM Treasury approved a business case for the reservicing of Buckingham Palace. The Trustees determined that it was appropriate to temporarily increase the percentage used to determine the Grant to fund the 10-year reservicing programme. Reservicing programme expenditure is set out within a framework agreement between the Royal Household and HM Treasury and limits the expenditure to £369 million (including VAT) to be spent over the 10 years to 2026-27. The Trustees' 2016 report noted that the government's intention to bring forward legislation to reset the level of the Grant to appropriate levels once the reservicing works have been completed. The phased programme of works started in April 2017. The latest periodic review of the Grant by the Trustees is expected to be published in 2023 and another review will occur in approximately five years, around the time the reservicing of Buckingham Palace should be completed.

Figure 4

The Crown Estate's revenue account profit and the Sovereign Grant, 2012-13 to 2022-23

From 2017-18, the Sovereign Grant increased by 10 percentage points from 15% to 25% of The Crown Estate's profit (from the revenue account) to cover the costs of the reservicing programme

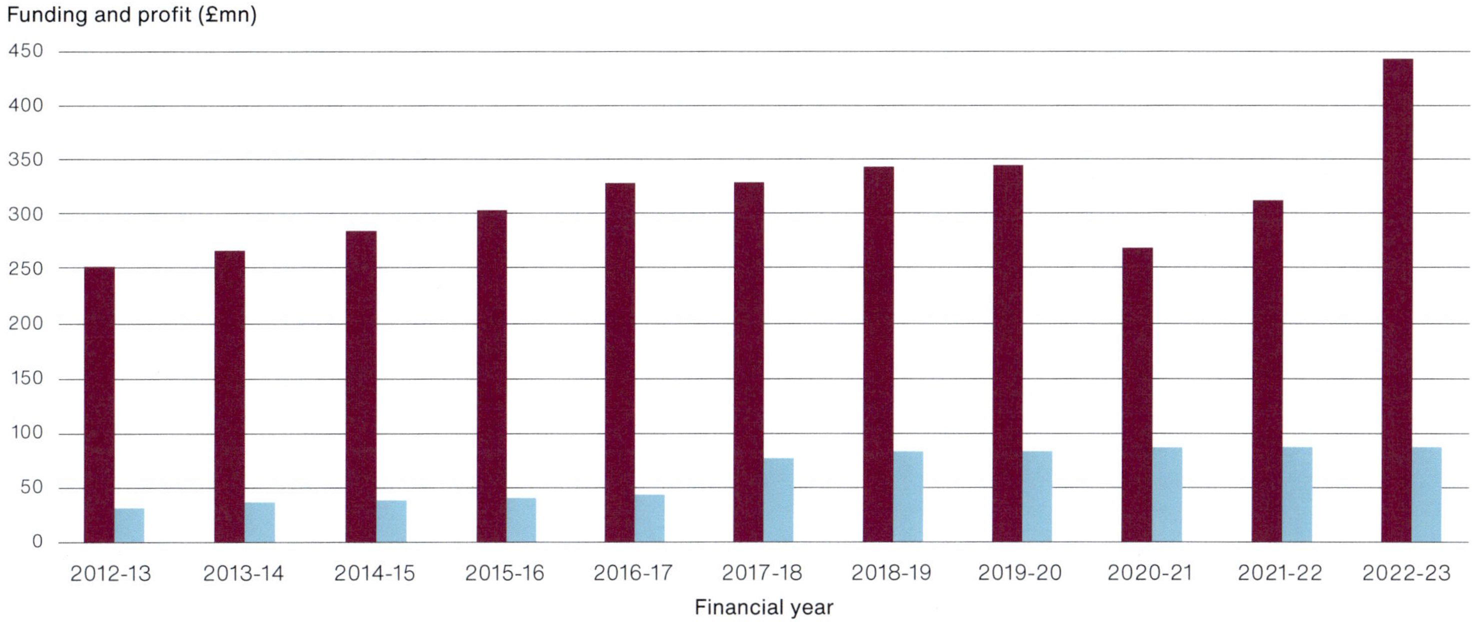

	2012-13	2013-14	2014-15	2015-16	2016-17	2017-18	2018-19	2019-20	2020-21	2021-22	2022-23
The Crown Estate's revenue account profit	252.6	267.1	285.1	304.1	328.8	329.4	343.5	345.0	269.3	312.7	442.6
Sovereign Grant	31.0	36.1	37.9	40.1	42.8	76.1	82.2	82.4	85.9	86.3	86.3

Notes

1 The Sovereign Grant (the Grant) is calculated as a percentage of The Crown Estate's revenue account profit two years prior. For instance, the 2014-15 Grant was based on The Crown Estate's revenue account profit in 2012-13.

2 Data shown are not adjusted for inflation as the Grant is based on the unadjusted revenue account profit two years prior.

3 The Crown Estate's revenue account profit for a financial year is stated in the statement of accounts certified by the Comptroller and Auditor General under section 2 of The Crown Estate Act 1961 (see section 12(1) of the 2011 act).

Source: National Audit Office analysis of The Crown Estate and the Sovereign Grant and Sovereign Grant Reserve annual reports and accounts

Figure 5

Options for reservicing of Buckingham Palace

In 2016, the Royal Household considered four options but ultimately decided on a different, hybrid plan

Option	Period (years)	Total capital cost (£mn)	Net present cost (£mn)
Full decant	6.5	360	278
Full occupation	21	374	246
Significant occupation	13	390	243
Partial occupation	8	353	232
Hybrid plan	**10**	**369**	**222**

Notes

1 Full decant involved completely relocating the Royal Household, including its staff, from Buckingham Palace for reservicing.

2 Full occupation involved reservicing Buckingham Palace while it remained fully occupied and functional.

3 The hybrid plan combined the significant occupation and partial occupation plans.

4 Net present cost includes adjustments for long-term savings, benefits and inflation.

5 The hybrid plan's net present cost was lower than any of the four original options because it provided several advantages, including minimal disruption to day-to-day operations and increased public access during the programme.

Source: National Audit Office analysis of Buckingham Palace reservicing programme summary report

1.14 As at 31 March 2023, the programme had received £199.7 million and spent £185.1 million, excluding capital expenditure of £15.4 million (**Figure 6**). The initial underspend of funding for reservicing was planned for by the Royal Household as it recognised that it would take several years for the project to get up to full speed. The Royal Household told us that the project is on track and is not expected to go over budget.

Sovereign Grant income and expenditure in 2022-23

1.15 In 2022-23, the Grant totalled £86.3 million (**Figure 7** on page 20 and **Figure 8** on page 21), of which £51.8 million was intended to cover core activities of the Royal Household and £34.5 million was intended to fund the Buckingham Palace reservicing programme. The Royal Household received £9.8 million in other income. An additional £21.2 million was drawn from the Reserve (Figure 7). The Reserve grew from 2017-18 to 2019-20 when the reservicing of Buckingham Palace was in its early stages and has decreased as the reservicing has progressed into the construction phases. The Reserve was £10.1 million as at 31 March 2023.

Figure 6

Funding and spending related to the reservicing of Buckingham Palace, 2017-18 to 2022-23

The reservicing grant has remained relatively stable over the years and additional costs have been covered by the Sovereign Grant Reserve

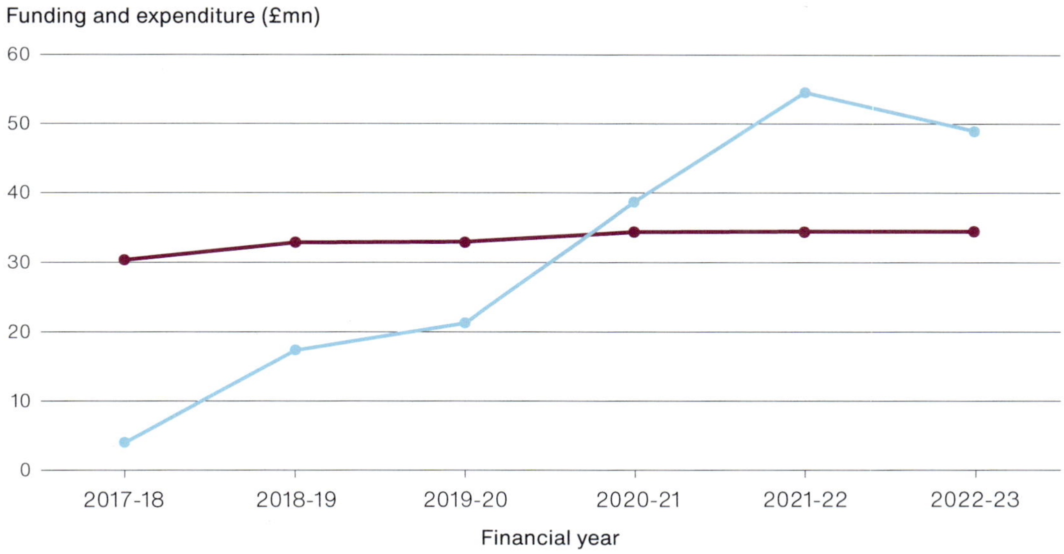

	2017-18	2018-19	2019-20	2020-21	2021-22	2022-23
Reservicing grant (£mn)	30.4	32.9	33.0	34.4	34.5	34.5
Reservicing spending (£mn)	4.1	17.4	21.3	38.8	54.6	49.0

Notes

1 Data shown are not adjusted for inflation.

2 When the grant exceeded spending, the surplus was deposited in the Sovereign Grant Reserve.

3 This figure includes revenue expenditure only. When capital expenditure is included, the Royal Household had spent all the funds allocated for the reservicing programme to 31 March 2023.

Source: National Audit Office analysis of Sovereign Grant and Sovereign Grant Reserve annual reports and accounts

Figure 7

Sovereign Grant-related expenditure and income, 2018-19 to 2022-23

In years when income does not cover Royal Household expenses, money is withdrawn from the Sovereign Grant Reserve (the Reserve)

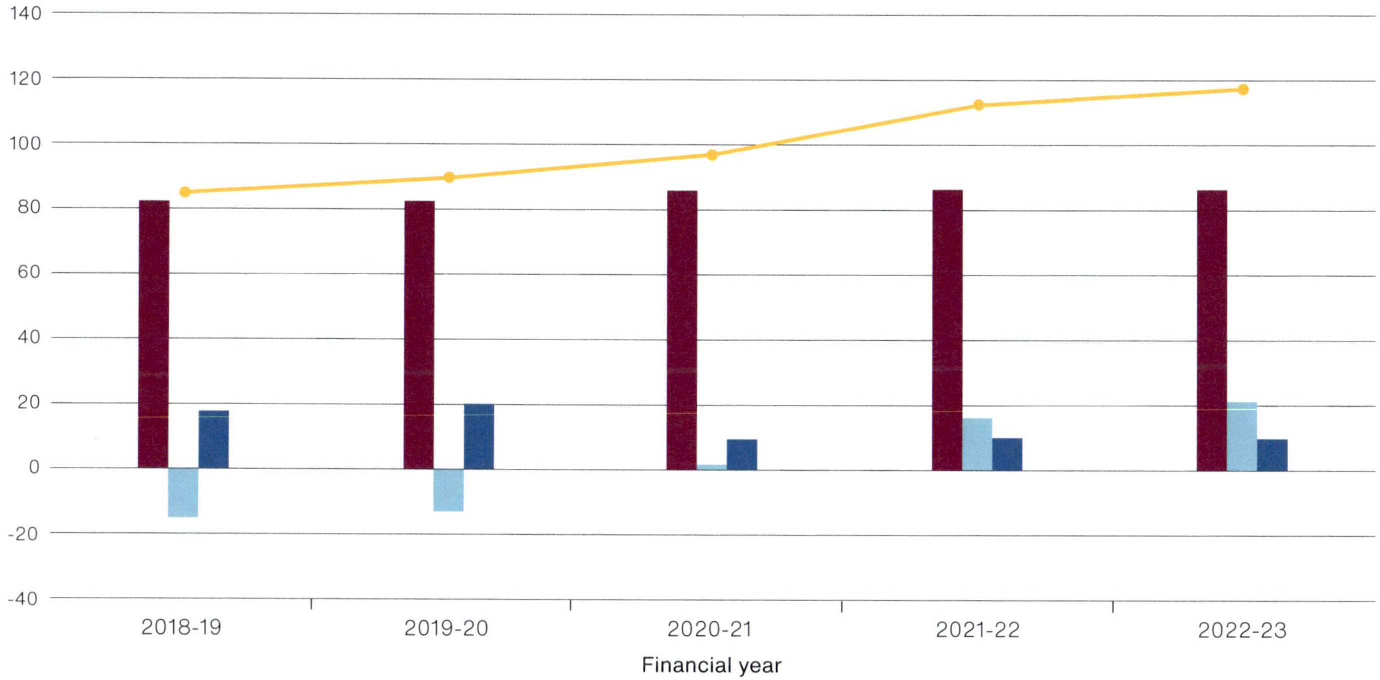

	2018-19	2019-20	2020-21	2021-22	2022-23
Sovereign Grant	82.2	82.4	85.9	86.3	86.3
Reserves	-15.2	-13.0	1.6	16.1	21.2
Other income	17.8	20.2	9.4	9.9	9.8
Expenditure	84.8	89.6	96.9	112.3	117.3

Notes

1 In any year, the Sovereign Grant, other income, and the Reserve transfer add up to the expenditure.

2 A positive reserves figure denotes the Royal Household drew down additional funds from the Reserve during the year to fund expenditure. A negative reserves figure indicates the yearly income from all sources exceeded the expenditure and a transfer was made into the Reserve.

3 Other income includes facilities management fees from the Royal Collection Trust, property rental income, and recharges for shared services and functions, and are reported in the Sovereign Grant and Sovereign Grant Reserve annual reports and accounts.

4 The Sovereign Grant Act 2011 sets out the expectation that the Reserve should be less than 50% of annual expenditure.

5 Figures are not adjusted for inflation.

Source: National Audit Office analysis of the Sovereign Grant and Sovereign Grant Reserve annual reports and accounts

Figure 8
Sovereign Grant income and expenditure, 2022-23

Property maintenance, including the reservicing of Buckingham Palace, is the Royal Household's greatest expense

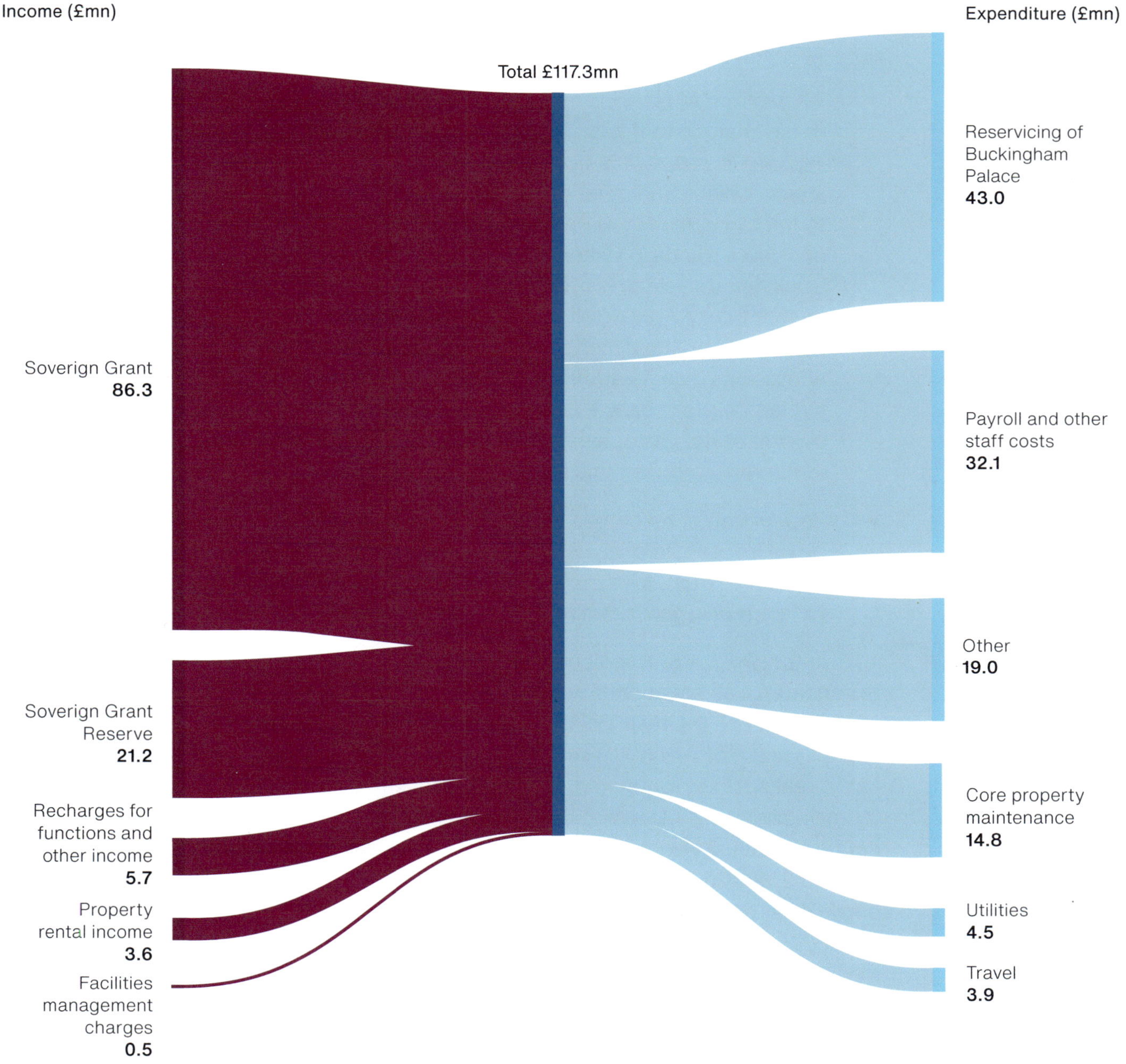

Note

1 Other expenses include housekeeping and hospitality, digital services and depreciation.

Source: National Audit Office analysis of the *Sovereign Grant and Sovereign Grant Reserve Annual Report and Accounts 2022-23*

1.16 In 2022-23, the Royal Household's £9.8 million in additional income consisted of:

- £3.6 million of property rental income. This rental income was received for the rental of properties in the Occupied Royal Palaces, including the letting of office space at St. James's Palace, Kensington Palace and Windsor Castle and residential space across all the Occupied Royal Palaces;
- £0.5 million of facilities management charges. The Royal Collection Trust paid these charges to the Grant for the purpose of maintaining the Occupied Royal Palaces. In return, it is permitted to occupy parts of those palaces for use as shops, offices and other purposes, including the admission of paying visitors to the Occupied Royal Palaces. These charges are based on a formula that considers trends in visitor numbers (at Windsor Castle) and how many days Buckingham Palace is open to the public for tours. The Royal Household told us that from 1 April 2023, the Royal Collection Trust's payment to the Royal Household will be either based on the pre-existing formula or 20% of the admissions income at Windsor Castle and Buckingham Palace, whichever is higher. This is usually the largest source of additional income but the enforced closure of the Occupied Royal Palaces during the COVID-19 pandemic temporarily reduced this stream of income; and
- £5.7 million of recharges and other income. Recharges refer to when the Royal Household charges another entity, such as the Privy Purse or the Royal Collection Trust, for services provided such as use of digital services. The basis for the recharges is outlined in the *Royal Household Treasury Finance Manual*.

1.17 In 2022-23, £57.8 million (49%) of the Grant and the Reserve's £117.3 million expenditure was spent on property maintenance (Figure 8). This included £43.0 million on the reservicing programme. In 2022-23, £4.3 million was spent on capital assets, of which £2.8 million related to the reservicing programme. Separate to the reservicing programme, the Royal Household also has a rolling 10-year plan for maintaining the Occupied Royal Palaces. Each year, this is broken down to create an annual works programme, which is funded by the Grant. Other significant costs in 2022-23 include: payroll (£27.1 million) for the salaries of Royal Household employees, who support the work of the Sovereign in their role as Head of State, and travel (£3.9 million) for official engagements in the UK and overseas undertaken by the Sovereign and other members of the Royal Family acting on their behalf.

Funding from the Duchies

1.18 The Sovereign receives income from the Duchy of Lancaster. The annual net surplus of the Duchy of Lancaster is paid to the Privy Purse and forms part of the Sovereign's private income. The Privy Purse funds official expenditure incurred by other members of the Royal Family who perform official duties that is not met by the Grant, at the discretion of the Sovereign. The Duchy of Lancaster is a landed estate held in trust for present and future Sovereigns since 1399. Its main purpose is to provide a private income for the Sovereign independent of both the Crown and the taxpayer. The Duchy manages an investment portfolio of land, property and financial investments. It also undertakes administrative duties associated with the area of the historical County Palatine of Lancaster (today, primarily Lancashire, Greater Manchester and Merseyside). Under the Crown Lands Act 1702, the Sovereign is only entitled to receive revenue (such as rental income) and not capital income (such as from the sale of land) from the estate, which is preserved to provide income for future Sovereigns.

1.19 The male heir to the throne, by virtue of holding the hereditary title of the Duke of Cornwall, receives income from the Duchy of Cornwall. This was established under the Great Charter of 1337. It is a private estate that provides income for the Duke of Cornwall (the male heir to the throne, also known as the Prince of Wales) and his family. The Duchy is governed by the Duchy of Cornwall Management Acts, which hold that the Duchy's assets are to be held for the benefit of present and future Dukes. As such, the Duke of Cornwall is entitled only to revenue income, the Duchy retains capital profits. Income from the estate is used to fund official, charitable and private expenditure of the Duke of Cornwall and his family. The estate is managed by the proper officers and the Prince's Council and its committees.[4] If there is no male heir the funds go to the Sovereign. If the funds go to the Sovereign, the Grant is reduced by that amount and HM Treasury would fund the female heir.

1.20 As neither the Duchy of Lancaster nor the Duchy of Cornwall are funded by public money, they are not audited by the National Audit Office. However, under the Duchies of Lancaster and Cornwall (Accounts) Act 1838, the accounts of both estates are laid before Parliament. This is facilitated by HM Treasury. The Treasury Officer of Accounts issues accounts directions to both Duchies, which stipulate the format and accounting standards for the accounts and a minister is required to lay both signed accounts before Parliament.

1.21 HM Treasury holds an additional statutory layer of oversight over the Duchy of Cornwall to ensure that the Duchy does not compromise the long-term value of the estate. The Duchy of Cornwall is required to obtain approval from HM Treasury for all property transactions above a set value. That value has changed over time and was £500,000 during 2022-23.

4 The four proper officers are: the Lord Warden of the Stannaries, the most senior position on the Council after the Duke of Cornwall, and deputy chair; the Receiver General, the non-executive chair of the Finance and Audit Committee, who has oversight of financial affairs; the Attorney General to the Duke of Cornwall, the principal legal officer; and the Secretary and Keeper of the Records, equivalent to the chief executive in other organisations.

Additional public expenses

1.22 At times, the Sovereign is involved in activities, such as ceremonial events and state visits, that are funded directly by government bodies or departments (**Figure 9**). Such expenditure is included within the financial statements of the relevant body. For UK government departments this expenditure is audited by the Comptroller and Auditor General in line with statutory departmental audit processes. Expenditure on these activities is not shown separately within departmental annual accounts. HM Treasury has confirmed that an estimated £161.7 million was spent by government departments and devolved administrations on Her Majesty the late Queen's funeral and related events. The numbers provided were marginal costs, meaning money spent specifically on the events, as opposed to costs that would have been incurred in any case.[5] Where necessary, additional funding was provided by HM Treasury to meet these costs. At present, an estimate of costs relating to the Coronation in May 2023 is not available. Any significant Coronation costs incurred by government departments will be included in their relevant future annual reports and accounts.

5 Hansard HC Written Statements, Volume 732, 18 May 2023. Available at Her Late Majesty Queen Elizabeth II: Funeral and Related Events- Hansard - UK Parliament (accessed 20 June 2023).

Figure 9

Activities funded outside of the Sovereign Grant

Some expenses related to the Royal Household are directly funded by government departments

Activity	Funded by	Expenditure information that is publicly available
Administration of honours	Cabinet Office	Not separately stated within the Cabinet Office's accounts.
Ceremonial occasions within the UK	Department for Culture, Media & Sport	Spend on ceremonial and cultural events amounted to £4.99 million in 2021-22. However, this includes other ceremonial events not related to the Royal Household.
Equerries and orderlies[1]	Ministry of Defence	Not separately stated within the Ministry of Defence's accounts.
Maintenance of the Palace of Holyroodhouse[2]	Historic Environment Scotland[3]	The Palace costs met by Historic Environment Scotland are covered within the annual grant-in-aid allocation and included as such in its annual report, but exact costs for Holyrood Palace and Gardens are not separately stated within its annual report.
Maintenance of Home Park at Windsor	The Crown Estate	Part of The Crown Estate's capital expenditure on the Rural Portfolio. Expenditure on maintenance of Home Park is not separately stated.
Security and police costs	Home Office	Not separately stated within the Home Office's accounts.
State visits by the Sovereign	Foreign, Commonwealth & Development Office	Not separately stated within the Foreign, Commonwealth & Development Office's accounts.

Notes

1 Equerries and orderlies are military officers who serve as attendants to the Sovereign.

2 Holyrood Abbey is a Property in Care. The properties in care estate are a collection of monuments, which define significant aspects of Scotland's history, brought into care for their long-term preservation and public benefit through the Ancient Monuments and Archaeological Areas Act 1979. The Palace and Gardens are maintained by Historic Environment Scotland but are operated commercially as a tourist attraction by Royal Collection Trust.

3 Historic Environment Scotland is partially funded by grant-in-aid from the Scottish Government and is therefore accountable to the Scottish Parliament. Its annual accounts are audited by an auditor appointed by the Auditor General for Scotland and the audited accounts are laid in Scottish Parliament in line with the Historic Environment Scotland Act 2014.

Source: National Audit Office analysis of the *Royal Household Treasury Finance Manual* and the annual reports and accounts of the departments and entities noted above

Part Two

Oversight and accountability

2.1 This part sets out the oversight arrangements that currently exist, including:

- internal governance and oversight arrangements for the Royal Household and the Sovereign Grant (the Grant);
- the respective roles and responsibilities of HM Treasury, the Comptroller and Auditor General (the C&AG) and Parliament;
- internal governance and oversight arrangements for The Crown Estate, including the respective roles and responsibilities of HM Treasury, the C&AG and Parliament; and
- the legal obligations of the private Duchies of Cornwall and Lancaster.

Internal oversight of the Grant

2.2 The Keeper of the Privy Purse and Treasurer to the Sovereign (the Keeper) is the Accounting Officer of the Grant and is accountable to HM Treasury and Parliament. The Keeper is responsible for the day-to-day operations and management of the Grant, and must:

- ensure that the Royal Household follows all necessary standards and requirements in the handling of public funds in order to safeguard the public funds in their charge;
- ensure the Grant is managed according to the required standards of governance, decision-making and financial management; and
- prepare an annual statement of accounts on the use of the Grant and supply a copy to the C&AG for audit.

2.3 Other responsibilities of the Keeper include signing the accounts, ensuring that proper records are kept and ensuring that they have been properly prepared and presented in accordance with the requirements issued by HM Treasury. They must sign a Statement of Accounting Officer's responsibilities and Governance Statement, commenting on the governance of the Grant and the system of internal control, for inclusion in the annual report and accounts. The Keeper must act in accordance with the terms of the framework agreement between HM Treasury and the Royal Household (see paragraphs 2.11 to 2.14), *Managing Public Money* and any other instructions and guidance issued by HM Treasury.[6] They must also assist the Permanent Secretary to HM Treasury and the Treasury Officer of Accounts on Grant matters that arise before the Committee of Public Accounts or other Parliamentary committees.

2.4 The Keeper delegates authority to the executive members of the Lord Chamberlain's Committee (the Committee), excluding the director of the separate Royal Collection Trust, to make decisions and incur expenditure in accordance with internally set delegation limits. Members of the Lord Chamberlain's Committee are the Lord Chamberlain, the heads of the Royal Household's five departments, the Private Secretary to Her Majesty and additional non-executive members.[7] It leads the Royal Household and has overall responsibility to manage its activities and is supported by several subsidiary boards and sub-committees, whose terms of reference are reviewed and approved by the Committee (**Figure 10** overleaf). This Committee:

- sets strategic plans and priorities and is responsible for monitoring risk, ensuring alignment with the desired performance and culture;
- oversees a risk management strategy that aims to ensure that risks are dealt with properly. The categories of main and emerging risks in 2021-22 included operational, financial, people, travel, fire safety and information risks;
- meets formally at least nine times a year; and
- has voluntarily adopted the UK corporate governance code.

6 HM Treasury, *Managing Public Money*, March 2022; HM Treasury, *Royal Household Framework Agreement relating to the Sovereign Grant*, March 2020; HM Treasury, *The Government Financial Reporting Manual: 2023-24*, December 2022.

7 The five collective departments that support the Sovereign and members of the Royal Family are the Private Secretary's Office, the Privy Purse and Treasurer's Office, the Master of the Household's Department, the Lord Chamberlain's Office and Royal Collection Trust.

Figure 10

Internal governance of the Royal Household including the Sovereign Grant

The Lord Chamberlain's Committee has overall responsibility for governance but delegates some authority to subsidiary boards and committees

Lord Chamberlain's Committee	Subsidiary boards and committees
Responsible for overall management and oversight of the Royal Household's activities, setting strategic plans and priorities, monitoring risk and ensuring that the Royal Household's obligations relating to the Sovereign Grant and to other stakeholders are met. It is also tasked with reviewing and approving the terms of reference for each of the Royal Household boards.	**Operations Committee** Responsible for the implementation of the strategic priorities and objectives of the Lord Chamberlain's Committee. Deals with operational functions from a strategic level.
	Risk Committee Responsible for the risk management framework for the Royal Household, assessing the scope and effectiveness of the systems established by management to identify, assess, manage and monitor financial and non-financial risks. Reviews the Royal Household's responsibilities, strategies, policies, conduct and performance of its risk management approach in respect of strategic and operational risks and assurance of the adequacy and effectiveness of the mitigation and control of risks. Supports risk owners to identify, assess and manage risk across the whole risk register.
	Buckingham Palace Reservicing Programme Executive Board (PEB) The principle programme board which overseas the delivery of the Royal Household's reservicing programme at Buckingham Palace. Chaired by the Master of the Household who is the senior responsible owner for the reservicing programme.
	Buckingham Palace Reservicing Programme Challenge Board Independently chaired and responsible for providing specialist scrutiny, oversight, advice and guidance to the PEB and the senior responsible owner as they work to deliver the reservicing programme.
	Security Risk Management Board Reports to the Lord Chamberlain's Committee, after considering reports from the Information, Personnel and Physical Security working groups.
	Aviation Safety Review Board Meets annually to consider the risks assessed by the Aviation Safety Management Committee on Fixed Wing aircraft and Helicopter travel.
	Audit and Risk Assurance Committee Oversees Royal Household's approach in regard to strategic processes, high-level controls, financial systems, sustainability, anti-fraud and both internal and external audit.

Note

1 Members of the Lord Chamberlain's Committee are the Lord Chamberlain, the heads of the Royal Household's five departments, the Private Secretary to Her Majesty and additional non-executive members.

Source: National Audit Office analysis of the Sovereign Grant's governance functions

2.5 The governance arrangements for the reservicing programme are set out in the framework agreement between the Royal Household and HM Treasury. They are designed to ensure proper oversight of programme risks and progress against targets. The main elements of the governance arrangements are:

- the Buckingham Palace Reservicing Programme Executive Board, which oversees the delivery of the programme. It is chaired by the Master of the Household who is the senior responsible owner for the programme and who, jointly with the Accounting Officer, is responsible for the delivery of the programme to cost, time and specification. Other members include senior management from the Royal Household, and an independent non-executive with extensive property project management experience;
- the Buckingham Palace Reservicing Programme Challenge Board, which provides specialist scrutiny, oversight, advice and guidance to the executive board. The independent chair of the challenge board has experience of managing large property projects. Other members include officials from HM Treasury and the Infrastructure and Projects Authority, and an independent non-executive who is a heritage buildings consultant;
- the Integrated Assurance Group which regularly reviews programme governance;
- formal Gateway Reviews and Checkpoint audits by independent reviewers. By 2023, seven programme assessment reviews and four gateway reviews had been completed; and
- the Grant's financial statements separately identify expenditure on core Grant activities and the reservicing programme, as required by the framework agreement with HM Treasury.

2.6 The Audit and Risk Assurance Committee of the Royal Household (Figure 10) is responsible for assessing the scope and effectiveness of the systems established by management to identify, assess, manage and monitor financial and non-financial risks. It is supported by the internal audit function, which is led by the Head of Audit Services. Members of the Audit and Risk Assurance Committee are independent non-executives chosen for their expertise in areas relevant to the Royal Household's activities such as business, technology, architecture, heritage buildings conservation and finance. They receive no remuneration in respect of their duties. Current board membership is disclosed in the Sovereign Grant and Sovereign Grant Reserve annual report and accounts.[8]

8 See page 40 of *The Sovereign Grant and Sovereign Grant Reserve Annual Report and Accounts 2022-23*, HC 1447, HM Treasury, June 2023.

2.7 The Audit and Risk Assurance Committee agrees a programme of internal audit work for each financial year. The Head of Audit Services compiles an annual report which provides an opinion on the Grant's controls environment and the adequacy of the systems and processes in place. This opinion is included in the governance statement within the annual report. The Audit and Risk Assurance Committee reviews internal audit findings and monitors progress on implementing any improvements that are required.

The roles of HM Treasury, the C&AG and Parliament in oversight of the Grant

2.8 The Sovereign Grant Act 2011 (the Act), which came into force in 2012, sets out the audit arrangements for the Royal Household and the Sovereign Grant Reserve (the Reserve) and also specifies external oversight (**Figure 11**). Proper accounting records relating to the Grant and the Reserve must be kept and statements of accounts must be prepared in line with requirements issued by HM Treasury, audited by the C&AG and laid in Parliament by HM Treasury.

HM Treasury's role

2.9 HM Treasury is accountable to Parliament for paying the Grant to the Royal Household. The value of the Grant is included in HM Treasury's budget, which is approved by Parliament in the annual Supply and Appropriation (Main Estimate) Act. The Permanent Secretary to the Treasury, as Principal Accounting Officer, is accountable to Parliament for the propriety and regularity of expenditure against HM Treasury's budget, which includes the Grant.

2.10 The Treasury Officer of Accounts coordinates with the Royal Trustees (the Trustees) to obtain approval for their annual report, alongside approval for access to the Reserve for specific pre-defined circumstances. HM Treasury approves the withdrawal of funds throughout the year in line with the ministerially approved conditions set out in this correspondence.

2.11 HM Treasury issues an accounts direction to the Royal Household in accordance with the framework agreement between the Royal Household and HM Treasury, which stipulates the format and accounting standards for the accounts. It states that the accounts shall be prepared in accordance with *The Government Financial Reporting Manual* as applicable to the Grant. The manual is a technical accounting guide for the preparation of government financial statements issued annually by HM Treasury. The accounts direction includes the information that the Grant's accounts are required to disclose, the exceptions to the requirements of the manual and additional disclosures that are required. The accounts direction is included as an appendix to the Sovereign Grant and Sovereign Grant Reserve annual reports and accounts.

Figure 11
External oversight of the Sovereign Grant and Sovereign Grant Reserve

Overall responsibility for oversight lies with Parliament, although HM Treasury, the Royal Trustees and the National Audit Office all have a role in oversight of the Sovereign Grant

Organisation	Roles and responsibilities
Parliament	Passes legislation.
HM Treasury	Specifies the format of annual report and accounts and has a framework agreement relating to the Sovereign Grant that sets out the governance and accountability arrangements between HM Treasury and the Royal Household. Pays the Sovereign Grant. Approves withdrawals from the Sovereign Grant Reserve. Lays the annual report and accounts before Parliament.
The Royal Trustees (Prime Minister, Chancellor of the Exchequer, Keeper of the Privy Purse and Treasurer to the Sovereign)	Calculate the annual Sovereign Grant. Hold unused funds as the Sovereign Grant Reserve. Review the level of the Sovereign Grant periodically.
The Royal Household	Supports the Sovereign to serve the nation. Maintains the Occupied Royal Palaces.
The National Audit Office	Audits the Sovereign Grant and Sovereign Grant Reserve annual report and accounts. May also carry out value-for-money examinations into economy, efficiency and effectiveness.

Source: National Audit Office analysis of the framework agreement between the Royal Household and HM Treasury relating to the Sovereign Grant

2.12 The published framework agreement sets out the governance and accountability arrangements between HM Treasury and the Royal Household including the specific responsibilities of the Permanent Secretary to the Treasury, the Treasury Officer of Accounts and the Keeper.[9] It is reviewed at the end of every review period, which is normally every five years.

2.13 The framework agreement states that the Royal Household:

- should follow the principles, rules, guidance, and advice in *Managing Public Money*, unless otherwise agreed by HM Treasury;
- provide an annual budget to HM Treasury for the forthcoming year as well as a three-year business plan; and
- provide HM Treasury with monthly management accounts and cashflow information.

9 *Royal Household Framework Agreement relating to the Sovereign Grant*. The framework agreement is available at: www.royal.uk/sites/default/files/media/sovereign_grant_framework_agreement_2020.pdf (viewed on 6 July 2023).

2.14 It also details how much and for what purpose the Royal Household can spend the Grant without HM Treasury approval. The spending limits and governance arrangements for the reservicing programme are also included within the framework agreement. HM Treasury approval must be sought for expenditure outside the delegations and for expenditure on policies which go against the principles of *Managing Public Money*.

2.15 HM Treasury appoints the Accounting Officer of the Grant and the Reserve, who is the Keeper. The Keeper is responsible for the day-to-day operations and management of the Grant, and ensuring the Grant is managed in line with the requirements set out in *Managing Public Money*. HM Treasury told us that the Keeper submits an annual letter of assurance confirming internal controls have been in place for the full financial year.

2.16 HM Treasury meet with the Royal Household every other month, and additionally as required, to discuss the monthly management accounts, changes to activities and procedures and ongoing approvals. HM Treasury also attends the Grant's Audit and Risk Assurance Committee meetings. The Treasury Officer of Accounts also sits on the Programme Challenge Board for the reservicing of Buckingham Palace.

2.17 The Royal Household produces a finance manual which sets out the expenditure met from the Grant and the circumstances under which costs can be charged to parts of the Royal Household including the Privy Purse, and the Royal Collection Trust and other households. This is updated annually and agreed with HM Treasury. It is also supplied to the Grant's Audit and Risk Assurance Committee annually for comment and information.

The C&AG's role

2.18 Under the Act, the C&AG audits, certifies and reports on the Royal Household's statement of accounts. The C&AG is the head of the National Audit Office (NAO). The C&AG's audit certificate and report is published within the Grant and Reserve annual report and accounts. The latest audited financial statements of the Grant and the Reserve were for the year ending 31 March 2023.

2.19 The accounts are prepared by the Keeper as Accounting Officer for the Grant and the Reserve. The framework agreement between HM Treasury and the Royal Household holds that the C&AG shares with HM Treasury any information emerging from the audit process, in particular issues relevant to HM Treasury's responsibilities related to financial systems within the Grant. This is shared through the reporting required under International Standards on Auditing to the Grant's Audit and Risk Assurance Committee.

2.20 Under the Act, the C&AG may also carry out value-for-money reviews – examinations into the economy, efficiency and effectiveness with which the Royal Household and the Trustees have used their resources in discharging their functions. The NAO previously reported on the Grant and its financial management in 2013. The C&AG plans to undertake audit work on the Buckingham Palace reservicing programme in 2024.

The Crown Estate

2.21 Under the terms of the Crown Estate Act of 1961, The Crown Estate is managed by a board of up to eight Crown Estate Commissioners (**Figure 12** overleaf). The duties of the Commissioners are to invest in and manage The Crown Estate's assets and to manage and enhance its value and the return obtained from it, with due regard to the requirements of good management. The board comprises seven independent non-executive board members and the chief executive. It currently has two board Counsellors. The board has delegated certain matters to four standing non-executive committees. The Commissioners are appointed by the Sovereign on the recommendation of the Prime Minister. The appointment of non-executive Commissioners is regulated by the Office of the Commissioner for Public Appointments (OCPA).

2.22 HM Treasury is The Crown Estate's responsible department and retains ultimate oversight of The Crown Estate. A framework document sets out how HM Treasury and The Crown Estate work together.[10] The Exchequer Secretary to the Treasury is the sponsoring minister for both The Crown Estate and the Royal Household and is answerable to Parliament. HM Treasury appoints the Accounting Officer for The Crown Estate, who is also The Crown Estate's chief executive. As The Crown Estate's Accounting Officer, the chief executive is bound by the requirements of HM Treasury's *Managing Public Money*.

2.23 The Crown Estate prepares an annual financial statement in accordance with the requirements of the Crown Estate Act 1961 and the accounts direction issued by HM Treasury. The Crown Estate's annual report and accounts are audited by the C&AG. The C&AG examines and certifies the accounts, which are laid before each House of Parliament by HM Treasury and may also carry out value-for-money reviews of The Crown Estate.

10 HM Treasury, *Framework Document: The Crown Estate*, June 2023.

Figure 12
The Crown Estate's governance

The Crown Estate's governance framework includes a central Board and non-executive board committees

Central board	Non-executive board committees
The Board Responsible for setting the objectives and overall strategy for The Crown Estate. It monitors financial performance and stewardship of The Crown Estate's assets and oversees the management of The Crown Estate's risks.	**Nominations Committee** Responsible for ensuring that the Board and its committees have the skills, experience and knowledge required to support The Crown Estate's strategy.
	Audit Committee Responsible for challenging and overseeing The Crown Estate's reporting, risk management framework, internal controls and policies and procedures.
	Remuneration Committee Responsible for ensuring that The Crown Estate's remuneration policies and practices support its long-term strategy.
	Sustainability Committee Responsible for ensuring that The Crown Estate's sustainability strategy incorporates best practice in environmental, social and corporate governance and is in line with The Crown Estate's values, principles and goals.

Source: National Audit Office analysis of *The Crown Estate Integrated Annual Report and Accounts 2021-22*

Oversight of the Duchies

The Duchy of Cornwall

2.24 The Duchy of Cornwall is a private estate established to provide an income for the present and future Dukes of Cornwall, independent of both the Crown and public support. As such, the Duchy does not manage public money. Under the Duchy of Cornwall Management Acts, HM Treasury must seek to ensure that the estate's capital is effectively protected for the benefit of future dukes.

2.25 HM Treasury and the Duchy of Cornwall publish a memorandum of understanding setting out the processes by which both bodies fulfil their respective legal obligations in relation to the management of the estate.[11] HM Treasury's remit is to:

- lay out the requirements for the Duchy's annual accounts. These requirements are updated periodically, in consultation with the Duchy;
- present the accounts before the House of Commons and the House of Lords so that Parliament can be satisfied that HM Treasury is fulfilling its statutory responsibilities; and
- approve large property transactions under the Duchy of Cornwall Act (1863) and approve other large transactions undertaken for the good of the estate under the Duchy of Cornwall Act (1982). The memorandum sets out the current limit under which the Duchy may undertake capital transactions without HM Treasury warrant approval. During 2022-23 this limit was £500,000.

The memorandum of understanding is reviewed every three years, with the latest review in August 2022.

2.26 The Duchy of Cornwall is not audited by the NAO as it is a private estate. The Duchy accounts are audited by external auditors as required by section 9 of the Duchy of Cornwall Management Act (1982).

Duchy of Lancaster

2.27 The Chancellor of the Duchy of Lancaster is responsible to the Sovereign for the administration (estates and rents) of the Duchy. Most recently, the Chancellor of the Duchy of Lancaster has been a member of the Cabinet Office and as such receives a ministerial salary under the Ministerial and other Salaries Act 1975. In line with other ministerial posts, they are appointed by the Sovereign on the advice of the Prime Minister. They are responsible to the Sovereign for the administration of the Duchy and may be called to Parliament to answer questions on the Duchy.

11 Duchy of Cornwall, *Memorandum of understanding between the Secretary and Keeper of Records of the Duchy of Cornwall and HM Treasury*, 4 August 2022.

2.28 Since 1 July 2000, each Chancellor of the Duchy of Lancaster has elected to revocably delegate all day-to-day administration of the estate to the Duchy Council except for specific powers relating to appointments. Appointments to the Council are made by the Sovereign on the recommendation of the Chancellor of the Duchy of Lancaster who obtains recommendations from the current Council. Council members include the chairman, the Receiver General (the Keeper), the Attorney General, the clerk of the council and chief executive officer of the Duchy of Lancaster. Other council members are chosen for their expertise or links to the County Palatine (see paragraph 1.18).

2.29 Under the Duchies of Lancaster and Cornwall (Accounts) Act 1838, the officers of the Duchy of Lancaster are responsible for preparing the annual report and accounts in accordance with HM Treasury's accounts direction. HM Treasury holds the responsibility for laying the annual report and accounts in Parliament. The Duchy of Lancaster is not audited by the NAO because it is a private estate and appoints its own external auditors in the same way as private UK companies.

Part Three

Future considerations

3.1 This part outlines future considerations (**Figure 13** overleaf) that may affect the Royal Household's funding arrangements, including:

- changes to The Crown Estate's revenue and net revenue profit arising from its trading activity, including from offshore windfarms;
- other factors such as the King's new programme, sustainability and inflation; and
- the current periodic review of the Sovereign Grant (the Grant).

Changes to The Crown Estate's revenue

3.2 The Crown Estate manages the seabed around the United Kingdom. It has the power to authorise programmes related to offshore wind energy, tidal energy, and offshore carbon capture and storage. The Crown Estate signed Agreements for Lease for Offshore Wind Leasing Round 4 in January 2023. Until they step into the lease or choose to exit the agreement, each project developer will be paying an annual fee to The Crown Estate to retain the option to build a windfarm. Approximately £1 billion of income per annum will be generated from the option fees across the six projects that comprise Round 4, for at least three years during the option period.

3.3 Once leases have been signed and construction begins on the new Round 4 offshore windfarms, The Crown Estate's windfarm-related income may decline.[12] If The Crown Estate's income falls, it may require another adjustment to the funding formula in the future. However, it is also possible that The Crown Estate's seabed rights might lead to additional sources of income.

3.4 Under the existing framework agreement between HM Treasury and The Crown Estate, The Crown Estate may annually transfer up to 27% of the previous year's revenue income to capital to support The Crown Estate's maintenance and investment programme.[13] An increase in the level of transfer would reduce the revenue account profit upon which the Grant calculation is based.

12 When individual projects meet all the relevant hurdles, the developers will enter into their leases and start to build their windfarms. At this point, the option fee income will cease and pre-generation rent commences at up to £25 million per annum across all six projects that comprise Round 4. Subject to the performance of other assets in its portfolio, The Crown Estate's income and net revenue profit could fall at the end of the Round 4 option period.

13 HM Treasury, *Framework Document: The Crown Estate*, June 2023.

Figure 13
Future considerations

Recent developments may alter future funding needs in substantial ways

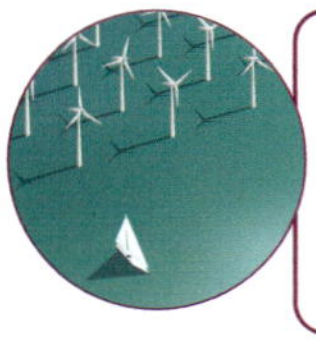

Windfarms

The Crown Estate concluded agreements for lease for six further offshore wind developments in January 2023, which will significantly increase The Crown Estate's profits.

The King's new programme

The new King will have a different schedule of activities from that of the late Queen.

Sustainability

Sustainability is one of the Royal Household's core strategic objectives and a priority for the government. The Royal Household has introduced a phased sustainability programme, with climate change the initial priority.

Inflation

Expenses and material costs have risen significantly in recent years, in line with rising inflation. This is of particular relevance to the ongoing reservicing of Buckingham Palace.

Source: National Audit Office analysis of The Crown Estate and Royal Household documents

Additional considerations

3.5 The King's future programme of activities has not yet been determined. Each King and Queen has their own interests and priorities which affect their schedule of events. Her late Majesty Queen Elizabeth II had cut back on events and travel in recent years, in part because of the global COVID-19 pandemic. It can be reasonably assumed that the King will be hosting more events and travelling to more engagements within the UK, and overseas at the request of the government. These changes may affect spending profiles but would be within available funding from the Grant. Parliament provided Prince Phillip with a separate annuity worth £359,000 per annum. Queen Camilla will not receive a separate annuity and the Queen's activities will be funded from the Grant.

3.6 The Royal Household outlined its sustainability agenda in its 2021-22 annual report.[14] That report contained an environmental review that discussed a range of plans to reduce greenhouse gas emissions, preserve nature and biodiversity, increase the use of sustainably sourced materials, water footprint the estate, and improve its environmental data collection. The report also described specific initiatives such as the installation of electric vehicle charging points, switching from gas lamps to LED lighting, and utilising biofuel.

3.7 The Royal Household has been developing its sustainability plan. Royal properties, many of which are historic listed buildings, present a number of sustainability challenges. As such, the Royal Household is consulting with external experts and partners to apply sustainability standards for historic buildings.

3.8 The Royal Household told us that it has appointed a sustainability lead and considered how best to implement its objectives. It is developing a sustainability programme with climate change as the priority area supported by six key areas of activity: calculating the Royal Household's carbon footprint; building a roadmap to Net Zero; enhancing internal and external communications; building staff engagement, knowledge and capability; establishing a governance framework and building appropriate external partnerships. These efforts build on the strategic aims that the Royal Household outlined in its 2021-22 annual report and it plans to implement its programme over the course of 2023-24. It told us that proposed decarbonisation options have been costed at a high level, with draft timelines for implementation which consider the expected profile of available funding, and feasibility studies will now be undertaken to provide more detailed costings and timings.

3.9 Inflation is also impacting on the Royal Household. The Royal Household has noted that due to the high inflation seen during the year, along with the death of Her late Majesty Queen Elizabeth II there has been increased pressure on the Sovereign Grant Reserve (the Reserve). Accordingly, the reservicing programme was reset to reduce the planned requirement to meet reservicing commitments from within the core Reserve in 2022-23. It does not believe this will impact on the overall completion of the programme as planned. The Royal Household had already altered its approach to the reservicing of Buckingham Palace because of the flat Grant in recent years and in 2023-24, delaying or altering some aspects of the original plan. For instance, it has dropped plans for an external visitor centre, determining that a more suitable solution is available inside Buckingham Palace.

14 *The Sovereign Grant and Sovereign Grant Reserve Annual Report and Accounts 2021-22*, HC 429, HM Treasury, June 2022.

Latest Royal Trustees' review

3.10 The most recent Royal Trustees' (the Trustees') review of the Grant began in 2021 and, as the Trustees decided to wait for greater clarity on The Crown Estate's future profits, in particular the timing of income from offshore windfarms, is expected to conclude in 2023. As part of the review, the Trustees will project income and expenditure to 2026-27. Revenue forecasting will be impacted by both the COVID-19 pandemic, which affected the profitability of The Crown Estate and income supplementing the Grant, and the additional income from Offshore Wind Leasing Round 4. Based on the current funding formula, the Grant would likely increase substantially if the formula is not revised, because of the additional income from Round 4.

3.11 If the Trustees determine that it is appropriate to reduce the percentage of The Crown Estate's revenue account profit used in the Grant funding formula, a statutory instrument will be laid in the House of Commons to give this legal effect. The Trustees are considering both core funding requirements of the Royal Household and the reservicing programme.

Appendix One

Our audit approach

Our evidence base

1 This report sets out Royal Household's financing and existing accountability arrangements. Our review took place between January and June 2023. The facts in the report are based on our three study questions:

- What is the role of public money in funding the Royal Household? This included differentiating between what is funded publicly and privately and determining the primary uses of public funds.
- What accountability and oversight arrangements are in place regarding royal finances, including the Duchies of Cornwall and Lancaster and the Sovereign Grant (the Grant)? This included analysis of the roles and responsibilities of HM Treasury, the National Audit Office (NAO) and the Royal Trustees (the Trustees).
- What are the future considerations that might impact on the Grant? This included a consideration of the ongoing reservicing of Buckingham Palace and the impact of offshore windfarm licensing.

2 We reviewed publicly available information relating to both the private and public funding of the Royal Household, however, we did not examine the private funding in detail. This report focuses on the Grant, which is managed by HM Treasury.

3 We have not conducted an evaluative review of the Grant and have not sought to make a value-for-money conclusion or to make recommendations.

Interviews

4 Our objective was to understand the roles and accountability arrangements for Royal Household funding. We had regular unstructured meetings with officials from the Royal Household and HM Treasury throughout the study, in which we discussed the topic and possible sources of evidence. Additionally, we carried out four semi-structured interviews on specific topics:

- the Royal Household's internal oversight and accountability arrangements;
- HM Treasury's oversight of the Duchy of Cornwall and Duchy of Lancaster;
- the Duchy of Lancaster's oversight and accountability arrangements; and
- the Royal Household's sustainability programme.

5 Interviews occurred online via Teams. Written notes were taken. Notes were analysed against our study questions and also analysed thematically for emerging themes.

Document review

6 We analysed past reports by the NAO and the Committee of Public Accounts on funding for the Royal Household. We sought to better understand the context of current arrangements, as well as changes over time.

7 Additional documents were collected using a variety of methods. We submitted a formal document request to the Royal Household and HM Treasury asking for copies of relevant documents. We also performed our own searches, using government websites and public tools such as Google. Furthermore, we commissioned research from legal experts to find all relevant laws and legislation.

8 We reviewed a range of publicly available documents in relation to Royal Household financing to help answer each of our main questions. The documents reviewed included but were not limited to:

- constitutional Acts governing the Grant;
- statutory instruments relating to the Grant;
- framework agreements;
- memoranda of understanding;
- annual report and accounts;
- public and Parliamentary correspondence;
- reports by the Trustees;

- published reports from The Crown Estate on windfarms; and
- a published report from the Royal Household on the reservicing of Buckingham Palace.

Analytical approach

9 We reviewed each document against our three study questions, with 18 sub-questions on the source, purpose, and oversight arrangements of the royal finances. Our analysis was used to inform further discussion and follow up with the relevant stakeholders.

10 We made use of expertise within the NAO to support our review and interpretation of documents. For example, we used our existing knowledge and evidence provided by the audited body, including our existing relationships and discussions with the Royal Household, The Crown Estate and HM Treasury.

Qualitative analysis

11 In general, the financial data in this report are in cash terms. They have been largely drawn from publicly available documents and referenced suitably throughout the report.

Limitations

12 Our report draws on information already in the public domain. Private details about the Royal Household are not publicly available and therefore not considered in our report. We have not reviewed oversight arrangements of private funding except to the extent that these procedures are performed by individuals serving within government departments.

13 We have not included a review of the tax status of the Royal Household or members of the Royal Family as part of this report.

Appendix Two

Legislation relevant to Royal Household funding, governance and oversight

Duchies of Lancaster and Cornwall (Accounts) Act 1838

It requires the Duchy of Cornwall and the Duchy of Lancaster to present their annual accounts to Parliament.

Duchy of Cornwall Management Act 1863

It sets the rules for the Duchy buying, selling and leasing properties. It lays out the warrant system, by which the Duchy is required to seek approval from HM Treasury for property disposals over a certain amount.

Duchy of Cornwall Management Act 1982

It widens the powers of management of the Duchy of Cornwall and specifies a new date for the date before which the Duchy's accounts are to be presented to Parliament under the Duchies of Lancaster and Cornwall (Accounts) Act 1838.

The Crown Estate Act 1961

It makes new provisions in place of previous Crown Lands Acts as to the powers exercisable by Crown Estate Commissioners for the management of The Crown Estate. It defines The Crown Estate as a 'body corporate' and sets out rules and requirements for the corporation to follow, including that accounts must follow the standards set by HM Treasury and must be audited by the Comptroller and Auditor General. It lays out the requirement to distinguish between capital and income accounts.

Energy Act 2004

It was a wide-ranging act that included provisions pertaining to nuclear power, gas and renewable energy. It includes a provision governing production of energy from water or winds in the British territorial sea and the Renewable Energy Zone.

Sovereign Grant Act 2011

It established a single grant to support the Sovereign in their official duties, replacing the previous system of grants and Civil List. It meets the central staff costs and running expenses of His Majesty's official household, covers maintenance of the Royal Palaces in England and the cost of travel to carry out royal engagements.

Made in the USA
Monee, IL
05 November 2026

67383065R00029